D1289286

United States Navy

RICHARD BARTLETT

Heinemann Library
Chicago, Illinois

Series designed by Heinemann Library
Page Layout by Herman Adler Design
Photo Research by Bill Broyles

Printed and bound in China
  by WKT Company Limited

08 07 06 05 04
10 9 8 7 6 5 4 3 2 1

Library of Congress Cataloging-in-Publication Data
Bartlett, Richard.
  United States Navy / by Richard Bartlett.
    p. cm. -- (U.S. Armed Forces)
Summary: Provides an overview of the United States Navy,
including its history, weapons, and vehicles.
Includes bibliographical references and index.
  ISBN 1-4034-0191-8 (Hardcover) -- ISBN 1-4034-0448-8
(Paperback)
  1. United States. Navy--Juvenile literature. [1. United States.
Navy.] I. Title. II. U.S. Armed Forces (Series)
  VA58.4.B37 2003
  359'.00973--dc21

                    2002015486

Acknowledgments
The author and publisher are grateful to the following for
permission to reproduce copyright material:
Cover photograph by Mason Cavazos/U.S. Navy
Title page, p. 30 Jim Hampshire/U.S. Navy; contents page,
pp. 4t, 7b, 27, 28, 31 U.S. Navy; p. 4b Kristi Earl/U.S. Navy;
p. 5t Steven G. Crawford/U.S. Navy; p. 5b Shannon
Renfroe/U.S. Navy; pp. 6t, 43 Defense Visual Information
Center; p. 6b Corbis; p. 7t James F. Gibson/The Library of
Congress; pp. 7c, 9, 10, 40 National Archives and Records
Administration; pp. 8, 41 Bettmann/Corbis; p. 11l Chris
Reynolds/U.S. Navy; p. 11r Corbis Sygma; pp. 12, 14, 15
Michael Worner/U. S. Navy; p. 13 Ralf-Finn Hestoft/Corbis
SABA; p. 16 Paul A. Souders/Corbis; p. 17t Anna
Clopet/Corbis; pp. 17b, 20, 23t Chris Desmond/U.S. Navy;
pp. 18, 37 Ramon Preciado/U.S. Navy; p. 19 Gary B.
Granger/U.S. Navy; p. 21 Don Smith/U.S. Navy; p. 22 Arlo
K. Abrahamson/U.S. Navy; p. 23b Andrew Mckaskle/U. S.
Navy; p. 24 Aaron Ansarov/U.S. Navy; p. 25t Mike
Stewart/Corbis Sygma; p. 25b Martin Maddock/U. S. Navy;
p. 26 Brien Aho/U.S. Navy; p. 29 Bob Houlihan/U.S. Navy;
p. 32 Alan D. Monyelle/U.S. Navy; p. 33t Angel Roman-
Otero/U.S. Navy; p. 33b Andrew Meyers/U.S. Navy; p. 34
Alex C. Witte/U. S. Navy; p. 35 Jessica Davis/U.S.Navy;
p. 36 Dwain Willis/U.S. Navy; p. 38 North Wind Picture
Archives; p. 39 Library of Congress; p. 42 U. S. Naval
Historical Center

Special thanks to Lt. Col. G.A. Lofaro for his review of
this book.

Every effort has been made to contact copyright holders
of any material reproduced in this book. Any omissions
will be rectified in subsequent printings if notice is given
to the publisher.

Some words are shown in bold, **like this.**
You can find out what they mean by
looking in the glossary.

Contents

Our Navy Today

The United States has the strongest navy in the world. Eight navy aircraft carrier **battle groups** carry more than 2,500 combat planes. The navy **fleet** of 72 submarines can fire torpedoes and missiles. The navy's 27 **cruisers** and 57 **destroyers** have missiles that can destroy enemy ships, planes, or ground troops. Fleets of supply ships support the warships. They deliver fuel, ammunition, food, clothing, and other things needed to help men and women on fighting ships do their jobs.

The United States Navy is a team. The team must always be ready to win a war. It must always be strong enough to convince other countries not to start a war. It must also keep ocean waters safe for ships of all nations. The navy's 295 ships and thousands of aircraft carry out these missions at sea each day.

This seal has been used by the Department of the Navy since 1957. The first seal was approved by the Continental Congress in 1780. There were two other designs before this one was approved by President Eisenhower.

The aircraft USS *Nimitz* (top), the fast combat support ship USS *Bridge* (middle), and the guided missile cruiser USS *Princeton* (bottom), were **deployed** in support of Operation Iraqi Freedom in 2003.

Leslie Scruggs, Information Systems Technician 3rd Class, stands watch with a machine gun on the USS *Mount Whitney*. Ship's Serviceman Seaman Brandon Banks reports what they see.

Working in the Navy

More than 350,000 men and women work in today's navy. That is more people than live in the city of Pittsburgh. About 55,000 navy men and women are officers. Officers give orders to the **enlisted** people. Every navy person is trained to do a certain job. Some operate **radar, sonar,** and weapons systems. Some people fly planes or helicopters. Other men and women handle supplies or cook food. Still others operate submarines. There are hundreds of different jobs in the navy.

Aircraft carriers are so big they look like floating airports. Carriers carry many kinds of aircraft, including fighter planes and helicopters.

Know It

The Department of the Navy is in charge of the regular navy, the navy reserve, the Marine Corps, and the Marine Corps reserve. In time of war, it is also in charge of the Coast Guard. The Navy Department's headquarters are in Washington, D.C.

The Navy Begins

In 1775 the thirteen colonies in America decided to break away from British rule. They were able to form a small army. But they did not have any ships strong enough to fight at sea. The British ships were stopping ships that carried food and other supplies the colonies needed. Ships in those days were built of wood and moved by sails.

The colonies changed small sailing ships, such as fishing boats, into fighting ships. Some of these won a battle against the British in Lake Champlain in New York. Then, French ships helped our navy break through a line of British ships at sea. Shortly after that, on October 13, 1775, Congress ordered that a navy of real fighting ships be built. That day was the birthday of the U.S. Navy.

Know It

The USS *Constitution* is the oldest commissioned warship afloat in the world. It's home port is Boston, Massachusetts. The people on her crew are on active duty in the U.S. Navy.

The officers and crew of the USS *Monocacy* sailed in 1871. The *Monocacy* was built in 1866. This ship sailed for almost forty years. Much of her service was in waters near Japan and China to protect ships carrying trade goods.

The USS *Constitution* was the first of the new ships added to our navy in 1797. It was called "Old Ironsides" because most bullets couldn't get through its thick oak **hull**.

In 1862 the sailors of the USS *Monitor* rested on the deck.

The ironclads

The first ironclad warships were built during the U.S. Civil War. They were the Confederate's *Virginia* and the Union's *Monitor*. Instead of being moved by sails, these ships had engines. Instead of wood hulls, they were built of iron. The two ironclads battled during the war, but neither could sink the other. Cannon balls bounced off both of them.

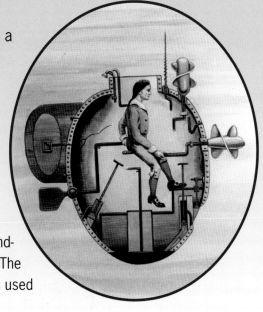

The *Saint Louis* was the first ironclad gunboat built in the United States. The *Monitor* and the *Merrimac*, which fought in 1862, were the first ships with iron hulls.

A Low-Tech Turtle

In 1776 the *Turtle* was the first submarine to go on a war mission. A propeller turned by hand moved the vessel. It was built of oak boards and had a large screw on top. The screw was supposed to drill into an enemy ship and make a hole big enough to place a bomb. *Turtle* tried to attack a British ship. But its screw could not drill through the hull.

The person inside the *Turtle* had to move it with a hand-operated propeller. This drawing was made in 1875. The screws in this picture are a bit different than the ones used on the real *Turtle*.

The first U.S. Navy submarine, the *Holland*, was bought by the navy on April 11, 1900. By the time World War I broke out in 1914, submarines were an important part of the navy **fleet**.

Steel and steam build a new navy

The first United States Navy warship built of steel and without sails, was the **cruiser**, USS *Charleston*. Congress ordered it to be built in 1885. Soon after, Congress ordered the building of nine battleships. The new navy **fleet** of big warships destroyed Spain's warship fleet during the Spanish-American war in 1898. This forced Spain to give up many of the islands it held near the United States. In the years that followed, the navy continued to grow. Cruisers, **destroyers**, submarines, and airplanes were added.

Telling Time at Sea

Navy ships use bells to tell time for sailors standing watch. This started in the days of sailing ships. In those years, most sailors did not have watches. A ship's boy kept time with a half-hour glass. This was a glass divided into two parts with a very narrow tube connecting the two parts. When it was turned upside down, the sand fell through the tube into the bottom half. Each half hour when the sand ran out, the boy would ring the bell.

The Navy during the World Wars

During World War I (1914–1918), navy ships fought battles with enemy ships and submarines. They also carried troops and supplies. This helped Britain and France fight the war in Europe. That war proved to American citizens that a strong navy was needed. The early air force showed that airplanes were also important in war. That led to the building of **aircraft carriers,** which allowed air planes to take off and land at sea. Other ships were built to supply and protect the carriers.

In World War II (1939–1945), American victories at sea against the Japanese Navy helped defeat the Japanese Empire. The planes that were based on navy aircraft carriers were important to these victories. Their bombs and torpedoes destroyed most of the Japanese fleet of warships.

During World Wars I and II, battleships like the USS *New Jersey* were the U.S. Navy's most powerful fighting ships. Today the navy does not use battleships.

Women in the Navy

For more than 100 years, only men served in the United States Navy. In 1908 the Navy Nurse Corps was formed. Until World War I (1914–1918), nurses were the only women in the navy. Then the war took thousands of men from navy jobs on land to serve at sea. Women took their places. Most of them worked as secretaries. Others had jobs as **translators,** fingerprint experts, navy **recruiters,** and hospital attendants. These women worked on land. Navy rules didn't allow women to work on ships. That changed in 1948, when women were allowed to serve on nonfighting ships. Women could then work on supply, transport, repair, and hospital ships.

These are the first navy nurses. They posed for this photo in 1908 in front of the Naval Hospital in Washington, D.C. They were nicknamed "The Sacred Twenty."

Making WAVES

Women who enlisted in the Navy during World War II were known as WAVES (Women Accepted for Volunteer Emergency Service). More than 26,000 WAVES served in naval aviation. They flew fighter planes and bombers to bases in the United States and Canada.

Frances Wills (left) and Harriet Ida Pickens became the U.S. Navy's first African-American WAVES officers in December 1944.

More Navy jobs for women

In 1978 women navy pilots were first allowed to fly support missions from **aircraft carriers.** Starting in 1992, women were allowed to work on all ships except **amphibious** vessels and submarines. Today women do almost all jobs in the navy. Thousands of navy women served in the 1991 Persian Gulf War.

They worked as air traffic controllers, mechanics, and radio operators. Some served on hospital, oiler, and ammunition ships. Others drove supply trucks.

The navy trains and places women in many important jobs. Here, Air Traffic Controller 3rd Class Samantha Sheran watches for aircraft returning to the *USS Bonhomme Richard.*

Loree Draude is one of the Navy officers who fly aircraft.

11

Boot Camp

Every **recruit** who joins the navy is given basic training. This takes place for nine weeks in the navy's boot camp. The camp is at the Great Lakes Naval Training Center on the shore of Lake Michigan in northern Illinois. Basic training teaches the recruit how to be a successful member of the navy. It is hard training. The recruit must get used to life away from home and obey strict rules.

A recruit is allowed to make one phone call home when he or she arrives. The next phone call is not allowed for weeks. They must always wear a navy uniform. Personal items brought to camp, such as radios or hair dryers, must be shipped home or given to charity. Use of tobacco, alcohol, or drugs by a recruit will get him or her kicked out of the navy.

Recruits read from the Bluejacket's Manual soon after arriving at the Great Lakes Naval Training Center. The first chapter they read is "From Civilian to Sailor." The manual was first written in 1902. It provides basic information to recruits. It has been updated many times as the navy has changed and become more modern.

Classes are part of a recruit's busy day. They learn about how to help the navy complete its missions. They are taught about navy vessels and the people and equipment that run them.

The first week

During the first week at boot camp, recruits fill out a lot of forms. They get physical and dental exams. They get shots for different diseases. They are given haircuts and swimming tests. Recruits who cannot swim are given lessons. There is physical training every day. Recruits also learn how to do things the navy way. They learn how to march. They learn how to salute, whom to salute, and who to call "sir" and "ma'am." They learn how to make a bunk and how and when to line up for meals.

Know It

The navy, like all of the U.S. military, works on a 24-hour clock. This is so that no one is confused about AM (morning) and PM (afternoon and night). The clock begins at 1 minute after midnight, which is written as 0001. It is spoken as zero, zero, zero, one. Noon is twelve-hundred (1200), and 1 PM is thirteen-hundred (twelve-hundred plus zero-one-hundred). The navy day ends at midnight, which is twenty-four-hundred hours.

In this training exercise, **recruits** must pretend that their ship is sinking and they must abandon ship. Once in the water, they must buddy up into teams, swim to the life raft, and climb onto the raft.

The toughest weeks

The first three weeks are the toughest for recruits. They have physical fitness training, marching, and classroom work. They also learn swimming, water survival, and fire fighting. This goes on from early in the morning until as late as 10 o'clock at night. Starting the third week of training, teams of recruits compete against each other. Those who do the best in their duties earn honor flags. This teaches recruits teamwork and the pride that comes from doing well.

Know It

Recruits must learn the language of the navy. For example, the front of a ship is the bow and the back is the stern. Looking toward the bow, the right side is starboard. The left side is port. The floors are decks, and the **hull** supports the decks. At the bottom of the hull, like a backbone, is the ship's keel.

The final tests

Recruits take a very difficult test near the end of basic training. It is called Battle Stations. The test starts at 10 at night and ends at 9:30 the next morning. Recruits must deal with emergencies like those that have actually happened on navy ships. They must show they can rescue crew members trapped by fire or explosions. They must show that they can put out fires. They must demonstrate that they know how to stop water from flooding a ship's hull. They must pretend to rescue crew mates from "dangerous" situations. Recruits must handle the tests as if they were real emergencies.

At the end of boot camp, recruits graduate. Each year the United States Navy graduates more than 54,000 men and women from basic training. The next stage of a recruit's training is for the job he or she will have while in the navy service.

Navy Officers

Today's navy has nearly 55,000 officers. They are the men and women in charge of seeing that the navy's missions are carried out. Men and women who have graduated from college can become navy officers by entering Officer Candidate School.

Children of people who have received the Medal of Honor (in any armed service) have automatic admission to any of the military academies.

The United States Naval Academy offers a college education as well as officer training. Students at the Academy are called midshipmen. They spend four years at the Academy. They must do well in classwork, physical training, leadership, and discipline. To learn teamwork, each midshipman must join an athletic program.

The Naval Academy graduates about 1,000 officers who serve in the navy and Marine Corps each year.

Know It

The president, a member of Congress, or the vice president must recommend a person who wants to attend the Naval Academy. He or she must be a high school graduate between the ages of 17 and 23. He or she must have good grades, be unmarried, and have no physical or behavior problems. Of the nearly 4,000 people recommended each year, only about 1,500 are chosen.

The Naval Academy is a four-year college. Every midshipman graduates with a bachelor of science degree. Those with top grades in their studies can choose to do graduate work before beginning their term of navy or Marine Corps service.

Choosing a navy job

Each midshipman must choose a subject to study at the Academy. This subject, or field of study, is important for the navy job he or she is interested in. There are 18 major fields a midshipman can choose from. These include mathematics, oceanography, computer science, and aerospace engineering.

Graduates of the Naval Academy can choose from many types of navy service. They might choose nursing, aviation, submarines, Special Operations Forces, or the U.S. Marine Corps. Within each service are many types of jobs. Graduates entering navy service are **commissioned** as ensigns, the lowest ranking officers. Those going into the Marine Corps are 2nd lieutenants. Each new officer must spend at least five years in the navy or Marine Corps.

An education in skills needed in the navy continues after graduation. This virtual reality trainer helps teach Landing Signals Officers how to guide planes and helicopters on aircraft **carriers.**

The Enlisted Force

Men and women below the rank of officer make up the **enlisted** force. There are about 325,000 enlisted **personnel** in the navy. They are the people who work at daily jobs that keep ships, submarines, and aircraft running smoothly. All enlisted men and women receive their basic training at Great Lakes Naval Training Center. When they complete basic training, they enter training for the special jobs they will have in the navy. The jobs could be on navy bases on land or at sea on ships or submarines.

Enlisted men and women work as aircraft mechanics. These Aviation Machinist's Mates are fixing the engine from a Sea Hawk helicopter.

In addition to navy personnel on active duty, more than 150,000 people are members of the United States Navy Reserve. These men and women train part-time. They can be called to active duty at any time. Some become part of the Reserve when they finish their active duty. Others join for the special job training the navy offers.

Electronics jobs

Electronic systems are part of all navy ships, submarines, and aircraft. Enlisted men and women operate most of them. They watch the sky and water with **radar** and **sonar** for enemy vessels and aircraft. Teams direct **missiles** and **torpedoes** to their targets. Others operate **navigation** and medical systems. Some enlisted men and women operate radios and code machines. They also help operate the navy's worldwide satellite **communications.**

Computer workers prepare all of these different electronic systems for navy missions. They also collect, study, and store information the navy needs to do its job. To make sure all these systems are working right, there must be teams to test them and make needed repairs.

On board the USS *Essex* near Japan, an air traffic controller monitors the radar system that tracks the ship's aircraft.

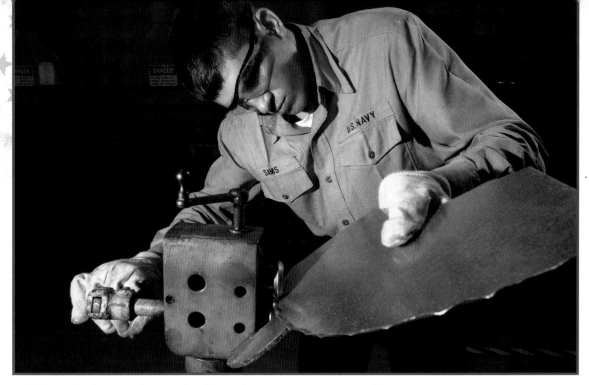

This sailor is a student at the Naval Construction Training Center. He is using a tool called a 90-degree elbow to bend a piece of sheet metal.

Construction jobs

The United States navy builds, remodels, and takes care of its property all over the world. **Enlisted** men and women operate heavy machinery. They might operate trucks, bulldozers, cranes, backhoes, or forklifts. They make airstrips and many kinds of buildings. There are many different construction jobs.

Some sailors have the job of telling the public about the navy. Photographers take pictures and make videos to send to newspapers, magazines, and television stations. Writers make captions and stories to send with the photos and videos. Some sailors prepare and present news and music programs. Translators put navy stories into foreign languages.

Some sailors make charts and blueprints and help prepare engineering plans. Some sailors install lighting, plumbing, heating, and air conditioning. There are other jobs for concrete workers, carpenters, roofers, wallboard installers, and painters. Sailors can also be part of rescue and rebuilding teams. They go to places damaged by floods or earthquakes.

On ship and shore

Enlisted men and women have jobs above and below a ship's decks. They operate and repair ship engines. They load and unload supplies. There are teams to repair, load, and fire a ship's guns. Other teams load and launch missiles and torpedoes. Some sailors fuel aircraft. Others help aircraft take off and land. Then they put the aircraft into storage hangars under the deck. Sailors in emergency units fight fires and go on sea and land rescue missions. Healthcare **personnel** help doctors, dentists, and nurses. They operate equipment such as X-ray machines. Navy cooks prepare and serve meals.

On land, members of the Shore Patrol make sure navy personnel obey laws and regulations. Human services specialists help navy members and their families with problems. For example, counselors help people who may have drug or alcohol problems.

More than 14,000 enlisted personnel serve in navy protective services jobs. The International Fire and Rescue Training Academy in Florida trains firefighters.

Navy Divers

The United States Navy leads the world in the development of diving operations. Diving has a long history in the navy.

Early divers

During the Civil War (1861–1865), divers were used to clear harbors of **mines.** But most diving work in those days was to help get back equipment from ships that had sunk in shallow water. Some divers wore goggles and had to hold their breath until they came back to the surface. Others wore heavy suits with helmets. The helmets had hoses attached to a boat on the surface. The boat pumped air to the diver so he could breathe underwater.

In 1912 diving suits and better equipment for breathing underwater were developed. These let divers work in deeper water and return safely to the surface. Soon after that, the submarine USS F-4 sank near Honolulu, Hawaii. Navy divers were able to go down 304 feet (93 meters) to help bring up the submarine and the bodies of its crew.

Today's deep sea diving suits have a lot of complicated equipment to keep divers safe. Often, another person must help the diver put the suit on and take it off.

Diver training

Most navy divers are trained at the Naval Diving and Salvage Training Center (NDSTC). It is located in Panama City, Florida. It trains all military divers except for those in the Special Operations Forces. This includes navy, army, air force, Coast Guard, and Marine Corps divers. The Center has 22 different courses with about 300 students at a time. It trains about 1,300 divers each year. Students study in classrooms and begin training in pools. They later train in St. Andrews Bay and the Gulf of Mexico.

These students at the Aviation Rescue Swimmer School learn techniques to save flight crews who crash into the ocean. They also rescue personnel who fall overboard at sea.

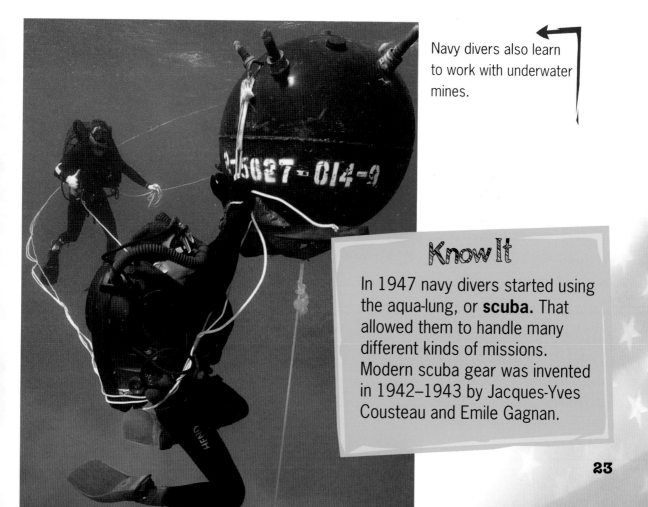

Navy divers also learn to work with underwater mines.

Know It

In 1947 navy divers started using the aqua-lung, or **scuba.** That allowed them to handle many different kinds of missions. Modern scuba gear was invented in 1942–1943 by Jacques-Yves Cousteau and Emile Gagnan.

This diver is wearing the Advanced Diving Suit. He is about to begin tests to find out what it is like to use the suit on a very long dive.

Navy divers have also worked with the space program. Early spacecraft were capsules that landed in the ocean. Navy divers would help astronauts into recovery helicopters. They would also attach cables to the capsules so they could be lifted aboard navy ships.

Today's divers

Navy divers now have many different missions. Some find and get rid of underwater **mines** and other enemy obstacles. They recover **torpedoes** that are fired for practice and research. Divers also do underwater construction and repair. They locate and recover downed airplanes and sunken ships. Other divers are part of the Special Operations Forces SEAL teams. SEAL stands for **SE**a, **A**ir, and **L**and. SEALs are trained to parachute, fire many kinds of weapons, and do hand-to-hand combat. They are experts in swimming and diving. One of their skills is to come from the water into enemy territory and carry out surprise attacks.

This is the navy's Deep Drone, an underwater robot.

Deep water

Many parts of the ocean are several miles deep. A diver cannot safely go to those places. So the navy has developed the Deep Submergence Rescue Vehicle (DSRV). The DSRV is operated by a crew of four. It is able to rescue crew members from a submarine in trouble. It can work at depths of 5,000 feet (more than 1,500 meters).

The navy also has Deep Drones. The Deep Drone is operated by remote control. It has cameras to find sunken ships or aircraft. Deep Drone can go as deep as 7,200 feet (almost 2,200 meters).

The USS *Monitor* was an important Civil War (1861–1865) ship. In 1862 it sank off the coast of North Carolina in 240 feet (73 meters) of water. Navy divers have recovered the ship's propeller, engine, and other parts. In 2002 navy divers began work on recovering the ship's turret and cannons.

The gun turret of the USS *Monitor* is lifted from the ocean floor 140 years after it sank. United States Navy divers worked with the National Oceanic and Atmospheric Administration to recover the turret and other parts of the *Monitor*.

The Navy's Animals

Animals have been used by military forces for thousands of years. Elephants, horses, and dogs have had a part in many wars. In 1959 the navy started its Marine Mammal Program. Marine mammals include dolphins, porpoises, whales, seals, and sea lions.

Dolphins

Research showed the navy that dolphins could help in underwater missions. They are very smart and can be easily trained. They can swim at high speed for many hours. They can also make deep dives. And most important, dolphins have a built-in system called echolocation to find things underwater. A program was started in 1962 to train dolphins to use this ability. The navy wanted to use them to find and recover underwater objects.

Another program in 1965 trained dolphins to bring tools and equipment from ships to divers working below.

Navy trainers work with dolphins like K-Dog. A signaling device is attached to K-Dog's flipper. This lets the trainer track him underwater. K-Dog is a bottlenose dolphin.

The tube containing the float that marks the mine's location can be seen attached to the dolphin's nose cap.

Mine-hunting dolphins

The navy has also trained dolphins to find **mines**. Dolphins use their **sonar** to locate fish in the water. So they are very good at finding mines. When it locates a mine, the dolphin swims close to it but never touches the mine. The dolphin is fitted with a nose cup attached to a tube. If it finds a mine, it drops its nose cup near the mine. The tube splits apart and sends a small anchor to the sea bottom. The tube also has a float attached to it with a line. The float goes to the surface. Navy divers go to the float. They follow the line down to the mine and take it apart.

During the Persian Gulf war in 1991, dolphins were used to find enemy mines and stray **torpedoes.** During the Iraq war in 2003, the navy took dolphins to the Iraq harbor of Umm Qasr. They helped divers clear the harbor so ships could safely dock with food and other supplies.

Dolphin relatives

Dolphins belong to a group of sea mammals called toothed whales. Other members of this family include beluga whales, killer whales, pilot whales, and porpoises. In the early days of the Marine Mammal program, many of these whales were tested for training. Some were used in studies to see if they could find downed pilots in the water. They were also studied to see if they could protect people in the water from sharks until they could be rescued.

Killer whales were trained in Hawaii by the navy. There the whales learned to bring back fake torpedoes from the ocean floor. The killer whale program no longer exists and the training facility has closed. There were only two whales in the program. One swam away when it was put into an open ocean training exercise. The other died after only five and a half years in captivity. Dolphins proved to be better suited for the program.

This orca is attaching recovery equipment to an object during training.

This is Zak, a California sea lion. Zak has been trained to find swimmers near piers and ships, who may be considered a threat to military forces in the area.

Sea lions

The navy also has a program for training sea lions. They have good eyesight in dim light and can dive deep. The navy is training sea lions to find enemy swimmers and divers. They are also being trained to find mines and to search for sunken ships and downed aircraft. After training, the sea lions are assigned to the Bahrain-based U.S. 5th **Fleet.** Then, they are tested to see how well they can work in the open ocean.

Navy pigeons

During the early 1900s, the navy had an enlisted rank for pigeon trainers. Their duties were to feed, train, and otherwise care for groups of homing pigeons. The pigeons were used to carry messages from ships back to land bases. In 1926 the navy had 12 lofts (pigeon houses) with about 800 birds.

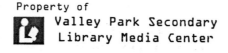

Navy Ships

The United States Navy has five **fleets** of ships. They are the 2nd, 3rd, 5th, 6th, and 7th fleets. The 2nd Fleet watches the Atlantic Ocean. The 3rd Fleet and 7th Fleet sail the Pacific and Indian Oceans. The 5th Fleet is in the Persian Gulf. And the 6th Fleet is in the Mediterranean Sea. Each fleet has fighting ships and support ships. Fighting ships are formed into **aircraft carrier** battle groups. Each carrier battle group has a Nimitz-class aircraft carrier. Two guided missile **cruisers,** a guided missile **destroyer,** a **frigate,** and two attack submarines protect the carrier. Sailing with the battle group is a combination ammunition-oiler-supply ship.

The USS *John F. Kennedy* participated in Operation Enduring Freedom in the Arabian Gulf in 2002.

Know It

The USS *Nimitz* is one of the navy's 14 aircraft carriers. It is the biggest ship in the world. It is as wide as a football field and $3\frac{1}{2}$ times as long. It has a crew of about 5,600 people. Like the other navy carriers, it carries up to 85 aircraft and is armed with guns and missiles.

The cruiser USS *Shiloh* launches a Tomahawk missile in 1996 in the northern Arabian Gulf.

Cruisers and destroyers

Battle groups' cruisers and destroyers are their bodyguards. These ships use **radar, sonar,** and aircraft to search the sea ahead of a battle group. They look for enemy planes, surface ships, and submarines. Cruisers and destroyers have missiles, torpedoes, and guns. They can direct their weapons at enemy aircraft, surface ships, and land targets.

A Tomahawk cruise missile is launched from a destroyer's vertical (straight up and down) launch system.

Cruisers and destroyers have three kinds of missiles. Standard missiles and vertical missiles are used against enemy surface ships and aircraft. Tomahawk missiles are fired against land targets. They can hit land targets as far away as 690 miles (1,110 kilometers). They were important weapons in the Persian Gulf and Iraq wars.

Below the water

The navy has three types of combat submarines. Attack submarines guard the waters around a battle group. They destroy enemy surface ships and submarines with Tomahawk missiles and torpedoes. Guided missile submarines also use Tomahawk missiles. They use them mainly against land targets. They can carry up to 154 missiles. Ballistic missile submarines warn an enemy not to fight with **nuclear weapons.** If it did, these submarines would hit back hard with Trident nuclear missiles. Trident missiles can hit targets as far away as 4,600 miles (7,400 kilometers).

The fast attack submarine USS *Salt Lake City* is next to the submarine tender USS *Frank Cable*. An attack submarine's engine is driven by steam produced by a nuclear reactor. This type of power lets the submarine patrol underwater without coming to the surface for up to three months.

A tender provides services to a submarine when it is away from its home port. The *Frank Cable* is one of only two submarine tenders.

The USS *Kearsarge* is an **amphibious** assault ship. It conducted support missions in Operation Iraqi Freedom (2003). The helicopters on its deck are Super Stallions.

Delivering the troops

Amphibious assault ships looks like small **aircraft carriers**. They carry marines and their equipment close to an enemy shore. Landing boats and helicopters take the marines from the ships to the beach. These ships can carry up to 1,900 marines. Its helicopters also help to unload their equipment. These ships are well armed. They have attack planes, missile launchers, and guns.

RHIBs can move in very shallow water. That lets them take a SEAL team to shore almost anywhere in the world.

Rigid **hull** inflatable boats (RHIBs) carry SEAL teams on secret missions. These are fast boats that can travel in rough seas and high winds. Because they are fast and small, they are hard for an enemy to detect. They have a crew of three and are armed with machine guns. RIBs can travel as far as 230 miles (370 kilometers) without refueling.

Other Equipment

The United States Navy uses more than just ships and sailors to protect our country. They also use aircraft and weapons.

In the air

Ships can carry more than 4,000 planes and helicopters. Some are used for moving troops and supplies. Others search for and attack the enemy. Most attack aircraft fly from carriers. These are F/A-18 Hornet and F-14 Tomcat jets. They launch **missiles** against enemy planes, surface ships, and land targets. The Hornet is also able to drop bombs and plant mines. Both of these jets had an important part in the defeat of Iraq in the 1991 Persian Gulf war and the 2003 Iraq war.

Another carrier-based plane is the S-3B Viking. This jet is used to look for and destroy enemy planes, ships, and submarines. It carries air-to-surface missiles, bombs, and **torpedoes.** It is also used to refuel other planes in the air.

The S-3B Viking can search the sky and water from 40,000 feet (about 12,200 meters) high during the day or at night.

The navy's Sea Stallion helicopter can deliver up to 37 battle-outfitted Marines to an attack area. The Sea Stallion has enough stretcher space to move 24 wounded people and four medical attendants. It can fly 665 miles (1,070 kilometers) without refueling.

Helicopters

Helicopters are very important to the navy. They need only a small section of a ship's deck to take off and land. They can **hover** when loading or unloading people or supplies. Helicopters are on **carriers, cruisers, destroyers,** and command ships. They are also on some support vessels such as **amphibious** assault ships. Helicopters fly troops and their equipment from ships to land. They also fly people from one ship to another. They deliver supplies to ships at sea and to troops on land. They take wounded troops to hospitals and rescue people.

The cruiser USS *Harry S. Truman* launches a Sea Sparrow missile. The Sea Sparrow missile can be fired in all kinds of weather and at different altitudes (heights). It can attack enemy aircraft and missiles from any direction.

Missiles

Big guns on battleships used to be the navy's mightiest fighting weapons. But battleships are no longer used. The big guns have been replaced by **missiles.** Missiles carry powerful explosives. They travel long distances and are very accurate. All navy **carriers, cruisers, destroyers,** submarines, and fighting aircraft are armed with missiles.

The navy has many different kinds of missiles. Harpoon, Penguin, Sidewinder, Phoenix, and Sea Sparrow missiles can be launched from ships or aircraft. Tomahawk missiles can be launched from surface ships or submarines. Trident nuclear missiles can be launched only from submarines.

Torpedoes and mines

Torpedoes can be fired from navy planes, ships, and submarines. Navy submarines carry MK-48 torpedoes. Cruisers, destroyers, and some planes and helicopters carry MK-46 torpedoes. Both kinds of torpedoes are designed to destroy surface ships and submarines. Torpedoes are only used against targets that are less than about 5 miles (8 kilometers) away.

Surface ships, aircraft, and submarines put navy mines in the water. They are used to destroy enemy ships. A ship doesn't have to hit a navy mine to explode it; the ship only has to come close. The mines are exploded by the change in water pressure from a nearby ship and by the sound waves coming from the ship's propeller. The navy has four types of mines. Two are for shallow water and two are for deep water.

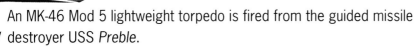

An MK-46 Mod 5 lightweight torpedo is fired from the guided missile destroyer USS *Preble*.

Famous Battles

The early years

The first navy sailing ships fought enemy ships with cannons. One of the most famous Revolutionary War (1775–1783) battles happened on September 23, 1779. Captain John Paul Jones challenged the British blockade with his ship *Bonhomme Richard.* He attacked the British ship *Serapis.* After more than an hour of close-up cannon fire, the British captain asked Jones to surrender. His answer was, "I have not yet begun to fight." Two hours later, the badly damaged *Serapis* was near sinking. The British captain surrendered. John Paul Jones became known as the Father of the American Navy.

In the War of 1812, the British tried to take over our country. They sent soldiers and war supplies from Canada across Lake Erie to Ohio. Our navy **fleet** was commanded by Oliver Hazard Perry. Perry's fleet destroyed the British ships. Then Perry helped chase the British back to Canada. This was a turning point in the war. Not long after, the British called for peace.

This engraving from 1779 shows the *Bonhomme Richard* battering the British ship *Serapis.*

Spanish-American War

By 1898 the United States Navy had a fleet of steel-hulled battleships, **cruisers,** and **destroyers.** That year, an explosion sunk the battleship USS *Maine* in the harbor at Havana, Cuba. At that time Spain ruled Cuba, Puerto Rico, and the Philippine Islands. The fate of the *Maine* was blamed on Spain.

The Spanish-American War began. A group of navy cruisers sailed to Manila Bay in the Philippines. They were commanded by Commodore George Dewey. Dewey's ships destroyed the Spanish fleet harbored there. Shortly after, a navy fleet commanded by Rear Admiral William Sampson sailed to Santiago, Cuba. They destroyed the Spanish fleet guarding the harbor there. That battle ended the war and gave the United States possession of Cuba, the Philippines, and Puerto Rico.

This portrait of Commodore George Dewey was done around 1898.

During their attack on Pearl Harbor, the Japanese sank or badly damaged 18 ships. The attack destroyed 188 aircraft and killed more than 2,200 sailors and soldiers. More than 1,100 of the dead were on the USS *Arizona*, shown here as she burned and sank.

World War II

The United States entered World War II (1939–1945) on December 7, 1941. On that day, Japan launched a sneak attack on the U.S. Navy **fleet** at Pearl Harbor, Hawaii. Then, the Japanese quickly captured some United States possessions in the Pacific, including the Philippines. Next, they planned to attack Australia. To have a base for that attack, the Japanese sent their fleet into the Coral Sea between New Guinea and Australia. On May 7, 1942, our navy met them. During the Pearl Harbor attack, our three **aircraft carriers** had been at sea. So they were not damaged. A two-day battle began between planes from American and Japanese aircraft carriers. It was the first naval battle ever fought with only planes. The Japanese fleet was forced to turn back.

The Japanese also made plans to attack Hawaii and then the west coast of the United States. To have a base close to Hawaii, the Japanese sent a force to take Midway Island in June 1942. Their ships included four aircraft carriers. A navy scout plane spotted the Japanese fleet. On June 4th, U.S. Navy planes from Midway and navy carriers attacked. They sunk all of the Japanese aircraft carriers and destroyed their planes. The remaining Japanese ships retreated.

Taking back the Philippines

In October 1944, the U.S. Army and Navy sent a force to take back the Philippines. They struck first at the island of Leyte. The Japanese knew that if they lost their bases in the Philippines, defeat was near. They sent forty-eight warships to stop the Americans. When the Japanese fleet entered Leyte Gulf, navy planes and ships' guns attacked. In a six-day battle, the navy sank three Japanese battleships, four carriers, and twenty-one other warships. Total defeat for Japan was then only months away.

In August, 1945, the U.S. Air Force dropped atomic bombs on two Japanese cities. This forced Japan to stop fighting. The official surrender took place in Tokyo Bay aboard the battleship USS *Missouri*.

A Navy of Change

Since its very first days, the United States Navy has worked to make itself better. Over the years it has built a **fleet** of powerful warships. It has also built ships to supply them. Navy aircraft have gone from clumsy biplanes to jets. **Missiles** have replaced big guns on warships and submarines.

Changes have also been made in who can be in the navy and what those people are allowed to do. In 1908 navy women were only allowed to serve as nurses. Since then, women have been accepted for almost every navy job. More opportunities have also been given to African Americans. Samuel Gravely, Jr. was a member of the Naval Reserve in 1942 when he was chosen for navy officer training. His superior work during his thirty-eight years in the navy earned him many promotions. From the lowest officer rank of ensign, he reached the top rank of admiral.

Samuel Gravely, Jr. was the first African American to become an officer from the Naval Reserve. He was also the first African-American commander of a major warship and the first to command a U.S. Fleet.

One part of the navy's plans for the future is the **stealth** test vessel *Sea Shadow*. The *Sea Shadow* was first shown in 1993–1994. The navy began using it again in 1999 for new tests and research.

The future

More changes that will make the navy better are going on now and will continue into the future. One navy program is called SEAPOWER 21. It includes better education for the navy's men and women and new ways to fight terrorism. The program also calls for improving the performances of the navy's ships, submarines, and aircraft. Changes have already been made to the F/A-18 Hornet fighter jet. Now named the Super Hornet, its new equipment makes it the best fighter jet in the world.

SEAPOWER 21 will add seventy-four new ships and submarines to the navy's **fleets.** The ship-building program has already started with the commissioning of three new **destroyers** and an attack submarine. Also, two of its current submarines are being changed so they can launch Tomahawk missiles and transport Special Operations Forces teams.

Sizing up the Navy

Organization of the Navy

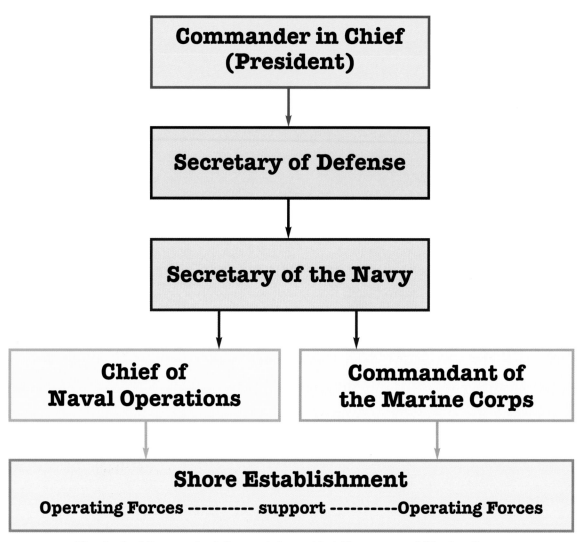

The dashed line marked *Support* shows that the navy and Marine Corps teams support each other.

Enlisted Occupational Groups	Examples
Administration	Recruiters, training specialists, instructors
Combat specialty	Special operations forces, weapons specialists
Construction	Crane operators, plumbers, electricians
Electronic and electrical repair	Computer repairers, weapons systems repairers
Engineering, science, and technical	Environmental health and safety specialists, intelligence specialists
Health care technicians	X-ray technicians, medical lab technicians, pharmacy
Human resource development	Chaplain assistants, caseworkers, counselors
Machine operator and precision work	Dental lab technicians, welders, metal workers, survival equipment specialists
Media and public relations	Photographers, audio and video editors, graphic artists, translators
Protective services	Shore patrol, law enforcement specialists, firefighters, military prison guard
Support services	Food service specialists
Transportation and material handling	Aircrew members, vehicle drivers, boat operators, cargo specialists
Vehicle and machinery mechanics	Aircraft mechanics, heating and cooling specialists, marine engine mechanics, powerhouse mechanics

Officer Occupational Groups	Examples
Combat specialty	Missile systems officers, special operations officers
Engineering, science, and technical	Communication centers officers, missile designers, pollution specialist officers
Executive, administrative, and managerial	Accountants, health administrators, purchasing managers
Healthcare	Nurses, physician assistants, physical therapists, dieticians, pharmacists
Health diagnosing and treating practitioner	Doctors, dentists, optometrists, psychologists
Human services	Social workers, chaplains
Media and public affairs	TV, radio, and movie directors, navy band director, public information officers
Transportation	Pilots, navigators, ship engineers

Glossary

aircraft carrier warship that has a deck where aircraft can take off and land

amphibious carried out by the action of land, sea, and air forces

battle group aircraft carrier and all the other ships that protect and support it during a war

communications sharing information

cruiser type of combat ship that mostly defends against attacks from the air

destroyer type of combat ship that mostly defends against attacks from the air. Destroyers carry torpedoes.

enlisted man or woman in the Navy who is not an officer

fleet group of warships under one command

frigate ship that escorts, or travels with, other ships

hover stay in one place while in the air

hull outer covering of a ship, usually made of metal or wood

mine container that holds explosives and is put underwater

missile rocket or bomb that is launched to destroy enemy planes, ships, or land targets

navigation process of steering a ship

nuclear weapon objects in fighting that explodes and gives off deadly energy

personnel people who work for a company or an organization

radar instrument that uses radio waves to locate objects in the air, on land, or on the surface of water

recruit person who has just joined the Navy

recruiter person whose job is to get people to join the Navy

scuba acronym for self-contained underwater breathing apparatus

sonar instrument that uses sound waves to locate objects underwater

torpedo large, cigar-shaped missile that contains explosives and travels underwater by its own power; used to blow up enemy ships and submarines

translator person who explains what is said or written in another language

More Books to Read

Abramovitz, Melissa. *The U.S. Navy at War.* Mankato, Minn.: Capstone High-Interest Books, 2002.

Bledsoe, Glen and Karen. *The Blue Angels: the U.S. Navy Flight Demonstration Squadron.* Mankato, Minn.: Capstone High-Interest Books, 2001.

Gaines, Ann Graham. *The Navy in Action.* Berkeley Heights, N.J.: Enslow Publishers, 2001.

Payment, Simone. *Navy SEALs: Special Operations for the U.S. Navy.* New York: Rosen Central, 2003.

Presnall, Judith Janda. *Navy Dolphins.* San Diego, Calif.: Kidhaven Press, 2002.

Index